Kites

written and illustrated
by Larry Kettelkamp

WILLIAM MORROW & COMPANY 1959

Flying for Fun

There is nothing quite like flying a kite. On a windy day the small, frail-looking form made of sticks and paper becomes a soaring bird. It dips and glides and may rise so high that it becomes a speck against the blue of the sky. It behaves like the hawklike bird which is called a kite and which gave the kite its name. Yet a single string, almost invisible, holds the kite steady, pulls it closer to the earth, or allows it more freedom.

On the ground a boy holds the other end of the string and feels the pull on the

3

line. The smooth performance of his kite is the result of many jobs well done. He built the kite carefully out of wood chosen for its strength and light weight, and he selected the proper covering material. He measured the parts of the kite accurately, cut the sticks, and sanded and balanced them. By using glue and special knots he gave the kite the strength it needed.

The boy who built the kite has also become an expert navigator. He has learned to estimate wind speeds, how to choose kite line, and what are the best ways of getting his kite safely into the air. He has learned why his kite flies and what the purpose of its tail is. He can take pride in its appearance and performance.

This book describes the basic types of kites and how to build and fly them for fun or in a tournament. It also tells of kites in other lands and of their practical uses.

Types of Kites

There are only two basic types of kites—those that are perfectly flat and have a single surface and those that are made of several surfaces which meet at an angle. The flat-surface kites need tails, while many of the angled kites can be flown without tails, if they are properly built.

Kites with angled surfaces fly with one edge leading into the wind. The surfaces slant back from this edge. If one surface swings around into the wind, the wind forces it back until both surfaces lead into the wind at about the same angle. In this way the kite corrects its position and can often remain steady even without a tail.

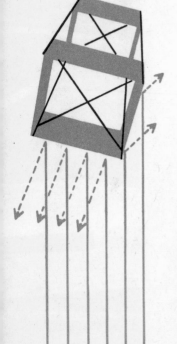

If angled kite turns, more wind strikes one surface more directly, forcing this surface back.

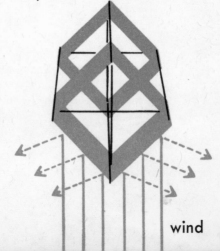

wind

wind

Building Kites

Many kinds of kites appear in hobby shops, dime stores, drugstores, and even grocery stores, during the months of March and April. While these kites do not cost a lot and are tested fliers, it is often more fun to build your own. You are the designer, builder, and navigator; the kite is your own from start to finish.

Materials for building kites are easy to find. Balsa wood, which is light and easy to cut and shape, can be bought at any hobby shop. Bamboo is also good, for it can be split into narrow strips. After it has been soaked in warm water, bamboo can be bent into many useful shapes. Pine, cypress, or spruce are stronger, and ideal for larger kites. These woods can often be bought at a hobby shop in strips about a yard long. Old Venetian blinds, lightweight fence pickets, or even packing crates may

balsa

pine

spruce

bamboo
sun curtain

bamboo
balloon
sticks

wooden packing
crate

supply wood which can be split or cut easily into narrow strips.

Tissue paper is the covering commonly used for kites sold in stores, and it works just as well for homemade kites. Newspaper and wrapping paper are heavier, but they will work too. Lightweight plastics and cellophane are also useful, and you can buy them at the ten-cent store. The plastics make vividly colored coverings, while the cellophane coverings have a transparent tint.

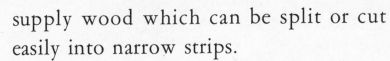

When splitting wood, never move the knife toward your hand or body. When sawing, keep your free hand out of the path of the saw.

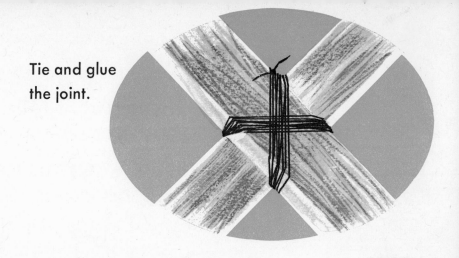

Tie and glue the joint.

Flat Kites

The kites made with two or three sticks are the easiest to build. The two-stick kite is made of sticks which cross in an X. The sticks of the kite shown in the drawing are 2 feet long, about ⅜ of an inch wide, and ⅛ of an inch thick. To fasten them together, wind string around the crossing and tie it tightly. Add household cement or airplane cement to the joint for strength. Never use tacks, for these may split the wood.

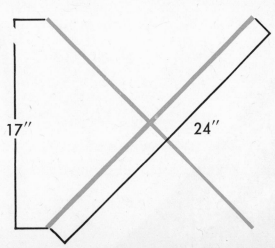

17" 24"

⅜"

⅛"

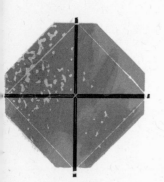

Fasten a string around the ends of the sticks to form the outer edge of the kite. To hold the string in place, cut notches in the sides of the sticks near each end, as shown in the drawing. Tie the string to each stick at the notch with a single loop knot. Pull the string tight between the ends of the sticks as you tie the knots. The distance from the end of one stick to the next should be about 17 inches.

Cut the covering material so that it extends about 2 inches beyond the area enclosed by the string on all sides. Fold the edges over the string all around the kite. If the covering is made of paper, fasten the folds with paper paste. Flour mixed with a little water makes a good paste. If the material is plastic or cellophane, use strips of cellophane tape instead of paste.

Decorating the Kite

If the kite covering is made of paper, you can design a pattern to decorate it. The cross sticks divide the kite into four triangles. If you paint each triangle a different color, you will get a geometric pattern.

Place some old newspapers under the kite before you begin to paint. Use water colors, liquid poster paints, or the poster paints that are made of powder and water

Apply glitter
paste evenly.

Sprinkle glitter
on wet paste.

Shake off extra
glitter when
paste is dry.

mixed together. Use a big brush and apply the paint gently so you do not tear the paper. The newspaper will absorb any paint that goes through the paper. As you paint, the paper will sag, but it will stretch tight on the kite frame as it dries.

You can also paint initials, faces, or animals on the paper covering with the water colors. Use broad strokes and keep the pattern or drawing simple. Remember, it will be seen most often from a distance.

The glitter sold in ten-cent stores makes good decoration. Decide which areas of the kite you want to decorate, and cover them with glitter paste or paper paste. Sprinkle the glitter evenly over these areas while the paste is still wet. After the paste is dry, shake off the extra glitter, and your design will appear. As the kite flies, the glitter will sparkle in the sunlight. The designs shown on the Oriental kites later in the book may suggest other ideas to you.

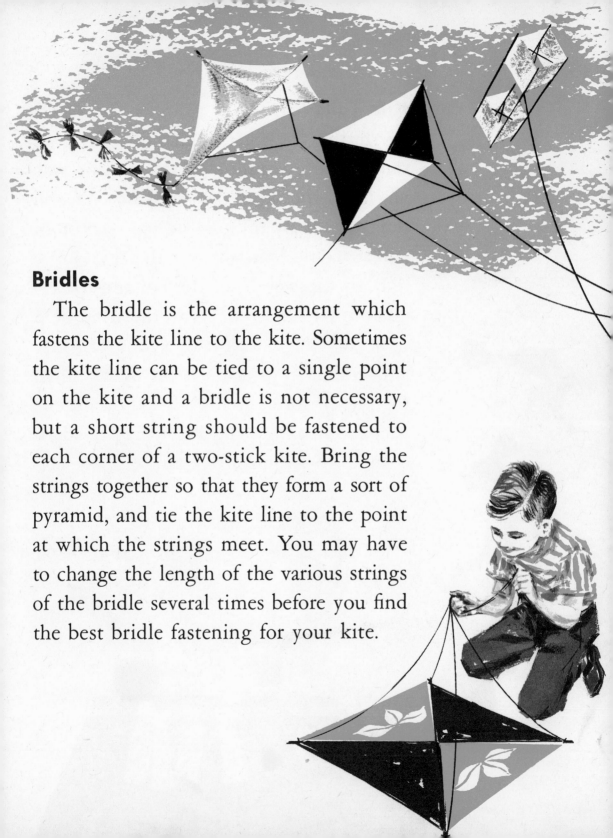

Bridles

The bridle is the arrangement which fastens the kite line to the kite. Sometimes the kite line can be tied to a single point on the kite and a bridle is not necessary, but a short string should be fastened to each corner of a two-stick kite. Bring the strings together so that they form a sort of pyramid, and tie the kite line to the point at which the strings meet. You may have to change the length of the various strings of the bridle several times before you find the best bridle fastening for your kite.

Kite Tails

All the flat kites need tails. Without one the kite would slip, first to one side and then the other, as the wind changed direction. It would have no top or bottom and it would spin all over the sky.

Both the weight of the tail and the resistance its surface offers to the wind help to steady the kite. Make a long tail first and gradually shorten it bit by bit until the kite performs well. As wind conditions vary from day to day, you may need to change the length of the tail.

If the kite dives, fasten a lead fishing sinker or metal washer to the end of the tail. When the kite dips, the tail will move to its proper position.

You can make a good tail from strips of cloth about 2 inches wide and 6 inches long. Tie them on a single length of string about 6 inches apart. Knot the string around the center of each cloth strip to hold it in place. This type of tail will offer as much resistance to the wind as one made of cloth strips tied end to end, and it will not weigh down the kite as much.

Paper cups tied to a string about 6 inches apart also make a fine tail, and it is light enough so that the kite can fly high.

36"

36" 8"

Malay kite

Angled Kites

One of the most popular angled kites is simply a variation of the two-stick kite. It is called the Malay kite or, after the man who developed an improved kite of this type, the Eddy kite. To build it, cross two sticks in the shape of a T. Add the string around the edge and the covering as you did on the two-stick kite. Now you will need to bow the stick which forms the cross of the T. Fasten a screw eye to each end of the cross stick by wrapping several turns of wire around the stick and the screw. Pull a string through the screw eyes and tighten it like a bowstring until the distance between the center of the string and the center of the stick is about ⅛ the length of the stick. Tie the string off tightly.

36"

4"

screw eye   screw eye

The measurements of the complete kite are shown in the drawing.

Because of the bow in the cross stick, the two sides of the kite form two surfaces which angle back slightly from the vertical stick of the T. Do not worry if the covering material sags slightly, for this will not hurt the performance of the kite.

This type of kite needs to be well balanced. The cross stick should be even in thickness. Measure it to find the exact center and rest the stick across a knife blade at this point. If it tips to one side, thin the heavy side slightly with sandpaper until it balances almost perfectly on the blade. If the kite is built with care, it may fly well without a tail. If it is not steady enough, add a tail, keeping it as short as possible.

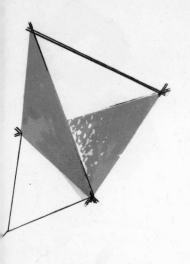

Tetrahedral Kites

The tetrahedral kite does not have the lifting power of the Malay, but it is a strong kite and flies steadily without a tail. Use 6 sticks 26 inches long, ¼ inch wide, and ¼ inch thick. Arrange them in the form of a pyramid with a base and three sides. Each side is the same size as the others, and each is an equal-sided triangle. Three sticks will meet at each corner. Use rubber bands to hold the corners in place temporarily. Cross the sticks so that about 1 inch of each stick projects beyond the crossing. Wrap string around each crossing, tie it, and add airplane glue for strength. Cover two sides and leave the other two open. When the kite is flying, the edge where the two covered surfaces

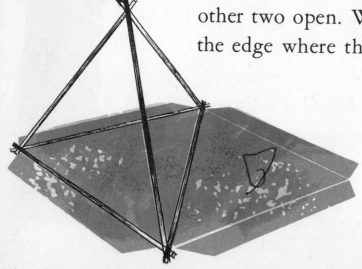

meet leads into the wind. Make the bridle by fastening one string to each end of the stick that forms this edge. Because the surfaces are sharply angled, this kite flies well in a strong breeze.

Box Kites

The most common box kite is an elongated box with open ends. Two separate bands of covering material are wrapped around the kite, one near each end.

To build this kite, you will need 4 sticks of spruce or pine 30 inches long, ¼ inch wide, and ¼ inch thick. You will also need 4 sticks for cross braces, each 17 ¼ inches long, ⅜ of an inch wide, and ⅛ of an inch thick.

Cut two strips of covering material, 50 inches long and 12 inches wide. Fold over 1 inch of each edge and paste it down. These folded edges will not rip and tear

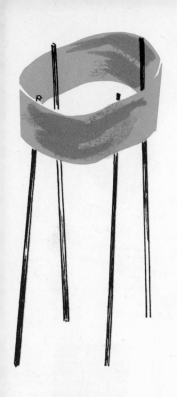

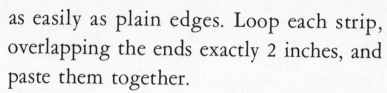

as easily as plain edges. Loop each strip, overlapping the ends exactly 2 inches, and paste them together.

Cut a V-shaped notch in the end of each cross stick, as shown in the drawing.

Using a ruler, make 4 marks, each 12 inches apart, along one long edge of both covering loops. Use household cement to glue the long sticks inside the loops at the marks, as shown in the drawing.

When the glue is dry, slip 2 cross braces into place 4 inches from each end of the long sticks, one set across the top and one across the bottom. The cross braces will bow slightly and will stretch the covering tight.

Attach the kite string to one long stick just below the top covering band. The kite needs no tail, since it flies edgewise into the wind with the leading surfaces angling backwards. It flies high and steady even in fairly strong winds.

Box kites can also have three, five, six, or more sides. You can use strips of bamboo that have been soaked in warm water and shaped into hoops, to build a box kite in the form of a cylinder.

You can also make kites that are variations of these basic types. Flat-surface kites can be built in the shape of stars, people, or animals. Larger tetrahedral kites, containing two, three, or more of the pyramid cells, can also be made. Flat-surface, tetrahedral, or box kites can be combined, so that the kite you make will seem to have sprouted wings of your own design.

shell of bamboo hoops and pine sticks for circular box kite

Extra Attachments

Once you have made a kite that is a good flier, you can perform some amazing stunts with it.

Punch a hole in a piece of paper, and cut a slit from the edge of the paper to the hole. Write a message on the paper. Slide the slot over the kite line, so that the line runs through the center hole. Bit by bit the wind will carry your message up the line until it reaches the kite. The wind will soon blow it off, and it will land on the ground far from the starting point. If you have written your name and address on the note, whoever finds it may return it or mail it back to you. Then you will know how far your message traveled.

A paper note, paper loops, and a balsa boat with pulley wheel can all be blown up the kite line by the wind.

If you have made a two-stick kite, you can add an extra stick between two of the spokes about 2 inches from the ends. Fasten the covering around this stick so the edge string is exposed above it. Now you can attach a musical hummer to this section of edge string. Cut a strip of the cover material, about 4 inches wide and a little shorter than the length of the exposed string. Fold the strip around the string and paste it together, so that it can turn freely around the string. Fly the kite with the hummer at the top and with the tail fastened to a loop of string tied between the lower spokes of the kite. When your kite is in the air, the wind will make the hummer vibrate.

Fold and paste.

You can also make a parachute for your kite line out of a handkerchief and a spool of number 10 thread. Tie a length of thread to each corner of the handkerchief and tie the free ends of the threads together beneath it. Also tie a small weight,

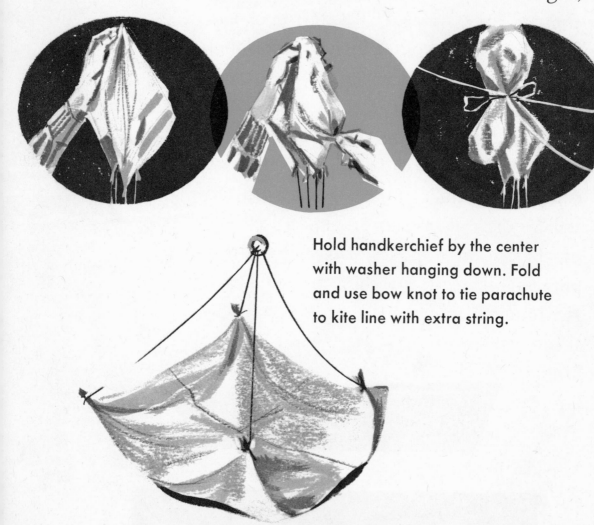

Hold handkerchief by the center with washer hanging down. Fold and use bow knot to tie parachute to kite line with extra string.

such as a metal washer, to the point at which the strings meet.

Make a number of parachutes of different colors, and fasten them along your kite line, so that when they are released, they will float down from high in the air. You will need an extra roll of string to fasten them properly. After your kite is launched, tie the first parachute to the line, using a bow knot, with the extra roll of string. Let out more kite line and more of the extra string together, allowing plenty of slack in the extra line. Tie the remaining parachutes on, with bow knots, at intervals in the same way. When all are high in the air, tug gently on the extra line, releasing the first parachute. As the parachutes fall, one by one, they will make a colorful sight.

Flying the Kites

The next time you ride in an automobile, hold your hand out the window with your palm down and your hand parallel to the ground. You will feel the pressure of the wind against your thumb and first finger, but your hand will stay in the same position. Now slowly rotate your hand, so that it is at an angle to the ground. It will tend to fly up and back.

Like your hand, a flying kite is held at an angle to the ground. It does not move through the air on its own power, but the wind that blows against it creates that effect. Some of the air spills over the top edge of the kite, while some flows downward along its surface. The air streams meet at the same time behind the lower edge of the kite. The air flowing over the top edge has a greater distance to travel in the same time, so it flows faster. Be-

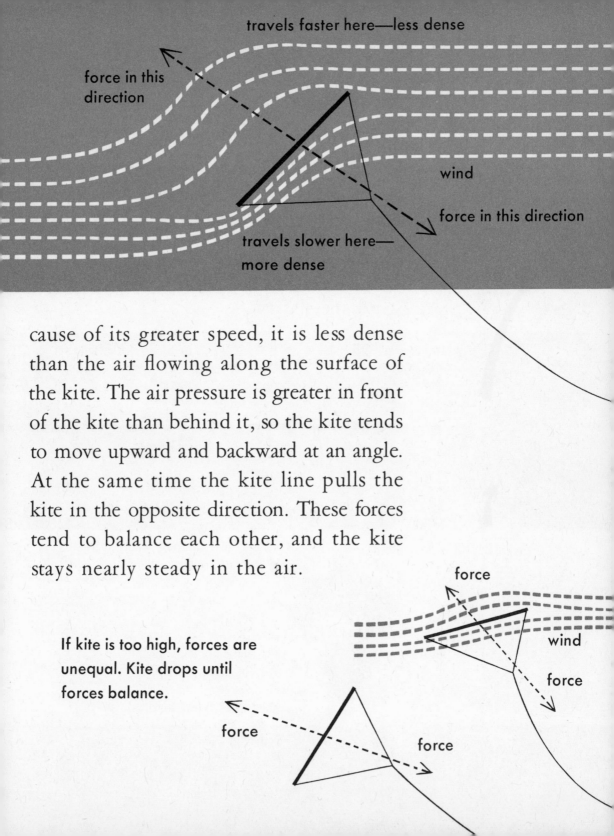

travels faster here—less dense

force in this
direction

wind

force in this direction

travels slower here—
more dense

cause of its greater speed, it is less dense than the air flowing along the surface of the kite. The air pressure is greater in front of the kite than behind it, so the kite tends to move upward and backward at an angle. At the same time the kite line pulls the kite in the opposite direction. These forces tend to balance each other, and the kite stays nearly steady in the air.

If kite is too high, forces are unequal. Kite drops until forces balance.

force

wind

force

force

force

Most kites need a wind of at least 4 miles an hour in order to fly at all. Winds of from 8 to 15 miles an hour should be ideal. Above 20 miles an hour the wind may become too strong for either the kite or the line. The Beaufort wind scale below will give you a key for estimating wind speeds.

Beaufort number	wind speed in miles per hour	These wind effects are from the Beaufort scale of wind force used by the U. S. Weather Bureau.
1	less than 1	calm, smoke rising straight up
2	1-3	weather vanes not moving, but smoke drifting
3	4-7	weather vanes moving, wind felt on face, leaves rustling
4	8-12	wind extending light flag, leaves and small twigs moving
5	13-18	dust and loose paper blowing, small branches moving
6	19-24	small trees in leaf starting to sway
7	25-31	telegraph wires whistling, umbrellas used with difficulty

safe for most kites

String and Reel

Rolls of cotton or nylon kite line can be bought at any hobby shop. Five-ply cotton wrapping string, fishing line, or tailor's button thread will also work for most small or medium-sized kites. Of course, if the wind is too strong, any string or thread may snap under the tension.

Since it is not easy to wrap and unwrap a tiny ball of kite line, a reel is a necessity if you plan to do much kite flying. The drawings show two simple reels. You can make the first from an old Ping-pong paddle and the other from wooden slats and dowels. To operate the paddle reel, hold it steady in one hand and pull in and wrap line with the other hand. The dowels used in the other reel serve as handles for both hands. Pull the reel close to your stomach, then extend your arms as you wind up several turns. This way you will avoid sudden strain on the line.

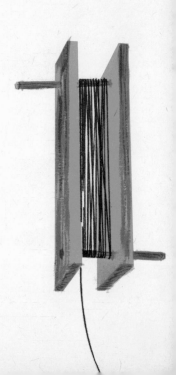

Launching the Kite

Here are some basic rules to follow when flying your kites. The more careful you are, the more you will enjoy your hobby.

1 Never use wire for a kite string.

2 Don't fly your kite near electric wires. If the kite gets caught in the wires, leave it there. It is better to make another than to risk an accident trying to free it.

3 Avoid flying your kite in city streets. Fly it in a vacant lot, playground, or open field.

4 Don't climb high trees or roof tops to rescue a kite that is caught.

5 Never fly your kite in the rain.

Houses and trees break up the force of the wind, making it hard to launch a kite. If possible, fly your kite on a level open field. The fewer trees there are, the less chance there will be of losing your kite in one of them.

Unroll about 75 feet of line. If you can get a helper, have him hold the kite as high as possible, at about its normal flying angle. If the kite has a tail, it should stretch away from you on the ground directly behind the kite. In this position it will help to balance the kite as it rises the first few feet.

As your helper releases the kite, back up slowly until the kite begins to rise, then gradually let out more line. If the launching is not successful, try unrolling either more or less string.

If you have no helper, you can still launch your kite. If there is a good wind and your kite is small, stand with your

31

back to the wind, holding the kite, by its lower corner or edge, in one hand and the kite reel in the other. When the wind seems steady, toss the kite gently upward at about its normal flying angle and step backward quickly. As the kite starts to rise, let out the line slowly. If you feed out too much line too quickly, the kite will not stay at the correct angle to the wind, and it will start to fall. If this happens, back up a few steps without letting out any more line.

If your kite is a large flat kite or a Malay, it may be too large to launch this way. Instead, place it face down on the ground with the top edge facing into the wind and the tail (if it has one) in a straight line along the ground away from

32

the wind. Unroll about 75 feet of line without disturbing the position of the kite. When you feel a good breeze, tug gently and step backward. The kite will tip up slightly, and the wind will move in between the kite and the ground, pressing against the surface of the kite.

To launch a box kite, stand it on end with the leading edge facing into the wind. As you step backward, the kite will tilt to the correct angle and rise a little off the ground. If there is enough wind, it will continue to rise and you can slowly let out more line.

If the wind is strong, but you still have difficulty getting your kite into the air, try adjusting the bridle or changing the length of the tail.

Kite Tournaments

March and April are the months for kite tournaments. Perhaps your town is enthusiastic about kite flying and already has a tournament. If not, you might have fun organizing a small one of your own.

Any tournament needs a group of events and rules for entering kites in each event. Those listed here are some of the most popular. The events can be as much fun for two or three people as for a larger group. Each person entering the flying events may have a helper for launching. **Design** This award can be given for decoration, the basic shape of the kite, and careful construction. No kite should qualify for the design award unless it can fly.

Altitude A fixed length of kite line, such as 200 yards, and a starting line are chosen. Each contestant begins flying his kite on the starting line at a signal. After a time limit, such as ten minutes, everyone must return to the starting line. The highest flying kite as seen from the starting line is the winner.

Speed Trip Each contestant has only 100 yards of kite line. He must send his kite out to the end of the line and reel it in again by hand. The kites are launched at a signal, and judges determine when each kite is at the end of its line. The first kite to return to the starting line wins.

Largest and Smallest Kites to Fly Successfully A minimum length of time should be selected during which a kite must remain in the air. Judges decide which kites stay in the air long enough for these events.

Message-Sending Race Participants take places along a starting line, and they send their kites out to the end of 100 yards of line. All messengers are released at a signal, and the first to reach the bridle of the kite wins.

A tournament tests all the skills used in building and flying kites, and it can be as much fun for the spectators as for those who are in it.

How Kites Began

It is not certain when or where kites were first developed. Some say kites were invented about 2400 years ago in Greece by a man named Archytas. The Chinese may have invented kites about 2200 years ago. Others believe that the first kites were flown on the islands off the tip of the Malay Peninsula about 2000 years ago. Wherever they may have appeared first, kites have been well known for centuries in the Orient, as far south as the island of Java and as far north as China and Japan.

風
箏

Chinese symbol
for *kite*

knife for tail
of Japanese
fighting kite

Oriental Kites

In Japan kite flying is a national sport. Contests are held in which prizes are given for design, construction, and accuracy of flight. Perhaps most exciting of all are the kite battles.

A special kite is built for fighting. It is a two-stick Malay type with a bowed cross stick, and its width is greater than its height. Paper tassels are attached to the corners. The kite is flown with a short tail, and it jumps or darts about in the air.

The owners add weapons to their kites for the fight. About 100 yards of the kite string starting from the kite are soaked in a sticky gum and dipped into powdered glass. When the gum has dried, this section of the line cuts like a saw blade.

A second weapon is made from a short piece of bamboo slit lengthwise in several places almost all the way from one end to the other. Curved blades of glass or metal

38

are pushed through these slits and tied tightly into place. Two of these knives may be added to the short tail of the kite, one at the end of the tail and the other about halfway down.

The opponents stand about 50 feet apart with their kites in the air. The object is to cut the opponent's string so that his kite falls to the ground. Fighting kites are flown low, so that they can be controlled quickly. Once a string is cut, the fight is over and the winner keeps both kites.

On May 5, the Boys' Festival in Japan, fish kites are fastened to bamboo poles outside Japanese homes. One kite is flown for each boy in the family. The kite is made of rice paper or cloth fastened to a hoop of bamboo which forms the mouth of the fish. It is hollow inside and even a light breeze will enter the open mouth of the fish. As the breeze blows through, the kite floats to one side of the pole. Some of

these kites are over 8 feet long, and each is carefully painted and decorated. There is a Japanese legend, which explains the origin of this celebration.

A Japanese boy named Kintaro once stood beside a river watching a group of fishermen. He saw a man-eating carp in the water, which was not noticed by any of the men. Quickly he threw himself into the water and fought with the fish until he had killed it, saving the fishermen.

In China kites are built to resemble animals of all sizes and kinds, both real and unreal. Butterflies, fish, frogs, centipedes, and even dragons may appear in the sky on a warm day, flown low enough so that all may see the details of the decorations of the kites.

A handsome kite is the Chinese butterfly kite. If you have two bamboo balloon sticks, you can make this kite. Soak the sticks in warm water. Bend each stick into

40

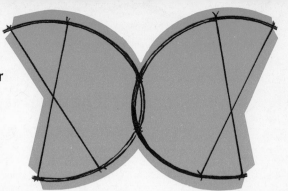

balloon stick frame
and covering pattern for
Chinese butterfly kite

a half circle. Fasten two strings to each stick, as shown in the drawing, to keep it curved. Overlap the sticks, as shown, and tie them tightly together. Add household cement to all the knots.

In China bamboo parchment is used to cover kites. You can use tissue paper. Cut the paper so that it is about an inch larger than the kite frame. Make slits an inch long along the curved edges of the paper with scissors. Fold the short tabs over the frame, and paste them down. Make the spots and marks of a butterfly with paint or pieces of colored paper pasted to the covering. Use a four-string bridle, tying each string to one end of a stick. Tie the tail to a loop fastened between the two lower ends of the sticks.

41

The largest Chinese kite is the dragon kite. It is not a single kite, but a series of a dozen kites or more linked together. The first kite, the head of the dragon, is large, and the others get smaller toward the tail. Bamboo sticks connect the edges of the kites. Once in the air, all sections tilt into the wind at the same angle, and the giant kite stays steady.

The dragon kite may belong to a society of Chinese gentlemen or to a workers' guild. It will certainly be launched on kite day, September 9.

Five or six men stand on the top of a treeless hill, holding the sections of the dragon kite above their heads and waiting for a signal from the man holding the kite string. Suddenly a gentle breeze rustles the sections of the dragon. The man with the string gives the signal, and the monster slowly rises as if waking from a deep sleep. Soon its head is high in the air, and its tail stretches above and behind it almost as far as the eye can see.

Useful Kites

Far from being only toys, kites have served many practical purposes. They were used to raise weather instruments for many of the first explorations of the air, they helped in the development of radio communications, and they suggested principles of heavier-than-air flight, which were used in building the first successful gliders and powered airplanes.

Exploring the Air

About 200 years ago, in Scotland, Alexander Wilson and Thomas Melville used kites to find out the temperature of the air above them. They sent up a train or series of kites. To each kite they attached a thermometer and a slow-burning fuse, which would cut the thermometer free from the kite once it had reached a certain height. As each thermometer fell, it trailed

44

a white-paper tassel so that it could be seen from a distance. The thermometers showed the temperature of the air at various altitudes.

About the same time, in America, Benjamin Franklin performed the now famous experiment in which he flew a kite during a thunderstorm. Electricity traveled along the wet kite line to a brass key, and sparks jumped from it to Franklin's hand. Although his experiment was dangerous, Franklin's kite proved helpful in answering questions about the nature of electricity.

About 70 years ago, before the invention of the airplane, William Eddy of New Jersey developed an improved tailless kite. In 1894 the United States Weather Bureau used five Eddy kites to lift a thermograph. This was the first time that a self-recording weather instrument had been lifted by a kite.

Soon a new kite became popular. This

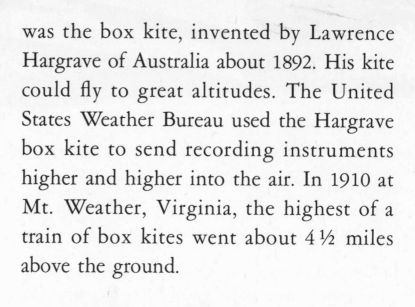

was the box kite, invented by Lawrence Hargrave of Australia about 1892. His kite could fly to great altitudes. The United States Weather Bureau used the Hargrave box kite to send recording instruments higher and higher into the air. In 1910 at Mt. Weather, Virginia, the highest of a train of box kites went about 4 ½ miles above the ground.

Kites to Airplanes

Alexander Graham Bell, the inventor of the telephone, also experimented with man-lifting kites. He developed a kite of his own, which he called a tetrahedral kite. It was built in the shape of a perfect pyramid, with two adjacent sides covered and two left open. He found that almost any number of pyramid-shaped cells could be joined together to make a steadier giant

Alexander Graham Bell's giant tetrahedral kite could lift a man.

kite with more lifting power. Bell built several tetrahedral kites large enough to lift a man. One of these was a giant made of 1300 cells. All the kites were strong and light, and Bell thought that men might be able to fly in them someday.

But it was the shape of the Hargrave box kite that the Wright brothers used in building their first glider. The glider, shaped like one cell of a box kite, was first flown as a kite. The Wrights also used the same box-kite shape to build their first motor-driven plane in 1903, the first heavier-than-air machine to fly successfully under its own power. Certainly the box kite fulfilled the hope of its inventor, Lawrence Hargrave, who had seen in it the possibilities of free flight.

the Wright brothers' first box-kite glider

Kites and Communications

Kites were also important in the development of radio communications. As a part of his experiments, Guglielmo Marconi used kites to raise receiving aerials above the ground. At Signal Hill, across the bay from St. John's, Newfoundland, Marconi fastened a wire aerial to a kite and flew it 400 feet high. The wire received a signal broadcast from Poldhu, England, the first radio signal ever sent across an ocean.

These men who experimented with kites used the kite as a tool for exploring new ideas. While you will build and fly your kites for fun, perhaps your hobby will have new meaning if you remember some of the accomplishments made possible through the study and use of kites.